Literacy Activity Bo

Year 2 Term 3

Louis Fidge

Letts

EDUCATIONAL

Acknowledgements
Everybody Said No! by Sheila Lavelle, published by A&C Black (Publishers) Ltd
Cats by Michaela Miller is reprinted by permission of Heinemann Educational Publishers, a division of Reed Educational & Professional Publishing Ltd
The Story of Dr Dolittle by Hugh Lofting © Hugh Lofting and published by permission of the Estate of Hugh Lofting c/o Ralph M Vicinanza, Ltd
Winnie-the-Pooh by A. A. Milne, published by Methuen Children's Books (a division of Egmont Children's Books Limited)
Veterinary Surgeon by Christopher Maynard from Jobs People Do, published by Dorling Kindersley Ltd
Silly Ghosts Gruff by Michael Rosen from Hairy Tales and Nursery Crimes, published by Scholastic Children's Books

First published 1998
Reprinted 1998, 1999

Letts Educational, Schools and Colleges Division,
9–15 Aldine Street, London W12 8AW
Tel: 020 8740 2270   Fax: 020 8740 2280

Text © Louis Fidge

Designed by Gecko Limited, Bicester, Oxon
Produced by Ken Vail Graphic Design, Cambridge
Colour reproduction by PDQ Repro Ltd, Bungay, Suffolk

Illustrations by Maggie Sayer, David Lock, Simon Girling & Associates (Sue King, Mark Ripley), John Plumb, Sarah Geeves, Graham-Cameron Illustration (Tim Archbold) and Karen Donnelly

British Library Cataloguing-in-Publication Data
A CIP record for this book is available from the British Library

ISBN 1-84085-185-6

Printed in Great Britain by Ashford Colour Press

Letts Educational is the trading name of BPP (Letts Educational) Ltd

Introduction

The Year 2 Literacy Textbooks:

- support the teaching of the Literacy Hour
- help meet the majority of the objectives of the National Literacy Strategy Framework
- are divided into three books, each containing one term's work
- contain ten units per term, each equivalent to a week's work

- provide one Self Assessment unit each term to check on progress
- contain one Writing Focus unit each term to support compositional writing
- provide coverage of a wide range of writing, both fiction and non-fiction as identified in the National Literacy Strategy Framework.

Unit number

Text for reading and discussion

Key teaching points

Text Level activities (purple)

Sentence Level activities (yellow)

Word Level activities (green)

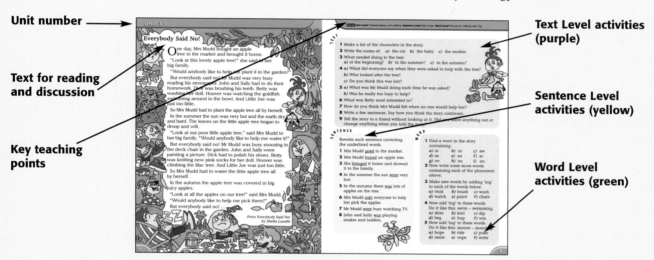

Writing focus unit:

- appears on pages 26–27
- develops work covered in the preceding ten teaching units
- supports work on compositional writing
- contains support for the teaching of different essential writing skills.

Self assessment unit:

- appears on pages 28–29
- reviews the key objectives at Sentence Level and Word Level in the preceding ten units
- contains a spelling chart to support the teaching of spelling strategies
- may be used to provide:
  - individual, group or class activities
  - a review of progress when completed and kept as a record
  - further practice in areas of concern
  - homework assignments.

The Glossary:

- contains and gives examples of key words and concepts
- contains illustrations to make meanings clearer where necessary
- may be used for teaching purposes or for reference by the pupil.

High frequency word list:

- contains words that occur frequently in children's reading and writing
- helps children to recognise these words on sight and spell them correctly
- is often referred to and used in the activities in the book
- provides an easily accessible resource for spelling activities and a ready reference section.

Focus		
Text Level	**Sentence Level**	**Word Level**
• Characterisation; oral retelling	Past tenses	Phonemes; suffixing with 'ing'
• Characterisation; settings	Commas in lists	Phoneme 'ea'
• Comparison with another author	Grammatical agreement	Words with the same spelling patterns/different sounds
• Responding to language play	Question marks	Thematic words; synonyms
• Characters; themes; comparison with another author	Questions	Suffixes 'ly' and 'ful'; digraphs
• Book blurbs	Turning statements into questions	Syllables
• Characters and settings	Standard forms of verbs	Spelling patterns
• Fiction/non-fiction; facts; use of headings	Posing questions	Thematic words; synonyms
• Contents page; index; glossary	Subject/verb agreement	Spelling strategies
• Evaluating text; comparing to original	Punctuation	Spelling strategies

Term 3

Writing Focus	*Finishing a story; Writing a story; Writing a nonsense verse; Writing an information text*

Self Assessment	*Review of Word and Sentence Level skills covered in Units 3.1–3.10 plus Handy hints for spelling words*

CONTENTS

Everybody Said No!

One day, Mrs Mudd bought an apple tree in the market and brought it home.

"Look at this lovely apple tree!" she said to her big family.

"Would anybody like to help me plant it in the garden?"

But everybody said no! Mr Mudd was very busy reading his newspaper. John and Sally had to do their homework. Dick was brushing his teeth. Betty was washing her doll. Hoover was watching the goldfish swimming around in the bowl. And Little Joe was just too little.

So Mrs Mudd had to plant the apple tree all by herself.

In the summer the sun was very hot and the earth dry and hard. The leaves on the little apple tree began to droop and wilt.

"Look at our poor little apple tree," said Mrs Mudd to her big family. "Would anybody like to help me water it?"

But everybody said no! Mr Mudd was busy snoozing in the deck chair in the garden. John and Sally were painting a picture. Dick had to polish his shoes. Betty was knitting new pink socks for her doll. Hoover was climbing the lilac tree. And Little Joe was just too little.

So Mrs Mudd had to water the little apple tree all by herself.

In the autumn the apple tree was covered in big juicy apples.

"Look at all the apples on our tree!" said Mrs Mudd.

"Would anybody like to help me pick them?"

But everybody said no! …

From Everybody Said No!
by Sheila Lavelle

TEXT

1 Make a list of the characters in the story.

2 Write the name of: **a)** the cat **b)** the baby **c)** the mother

3 What needed doing to the tree:
a) at the beginning? **b)** in the summer? **c)** in the autumn?

4 a) What did everyone say when they were asked to help with the tree?

b) Who looked after the tree?

c) Do you think this was fair?

5 a) What was Mr Mudd doing each time he was asked?

b) Was he really too busy to help?

6 What was Betty most interested in?

7 How do you think Mrs Mudd felt when no one would help her?

8 Write a few sentences. Say how you think the story continues.

9 Tell the story to a friend without looking at it. Did you leave anything out or change anything when you told the story?

SENTENCE

Rewrite each sentence correcting the underlined words.

1 Mrs Mudd <u>goed</u> to the market.

2 Mrs Mudd <u>buyed</u> an apple tree.

3 She <u>bringed</u> it home and showed it to the family.

4 In the summer the sun <u>were</u> very hot.

5 In the autumn there <u>was</u> lots of apples on the tree.

6 Mrs Mudd <u>askt</u> everyone to help her pick the apples.

7 Mr Mudd <u>were</u> busy watching TV.

8 John and Sally <u>was</u> playing snakes and ladders.

WORD

1 Find a word in the story containing:
a) ai **b)** ar **c)** ew
d) ee **e)** ea **f)** er
g) oo **h)** ou **i)** au

2 Now write some more words containing each of the phonemes above.

3 Make new words by adding 'ing' to each of the words below.
a) read **b)** brush **c)** wash
d) watch **e)** paint **f)** climb

4 Now add 'ing' to these words.
Do it like this: swim – swimming
a) skim **b)** knit **c)** dip
d) beg **e)** hop **f)** win

5 Now add 'ing' to these words.
Do it like this: snooze – snoozing
a) hope **b)** ride **c)** poke
d) smile **e)** wipe **f)** write

7

The Brute Family

In the middle of a dark and shadowy wood lived a little family of Brutes. There were Papa Brute, Mama Brute, Brother and Sister Brute and Baby Brute. Baby Brute howled between spoonfuls. Brother and Sister Brute kicked each other under the table, and Mama and Papa made faces while they ate.

After breakfast Papa Brute took up his sack and went off to gather sticks and stones. Mama stayed at home to thump the furniture and bang the pots and scold the baby. And Brother and Sister Brute pushed and shoved and punched and pinched their way to school.

In the evenings Mama served a stew of sticks and stones, and the family ate it with growls and grumblings. Then they groaned and went to sleep. That was how they lived. They never laughed and said, "Delightful!" They never smiled and said, "How lovely!"

... Then one day Baby Brute found a little lost wandering good feeling in a field of daisies, and he caught it up and put it in his tiny pocket. And he felt so good that he laughed and said, "How lovely."

From The Little Brute Family *by Russell Hoban*

TEXT

1 Where does the story take place?

2 Who are the main characters?

3 What does each character do during the day?

4 How did Brother and Sister Brute treat each other?

5 Write which of these words describe the Brutes:

cheerful	nasty
miserable	unfriendly
kind	unhappy

6 *a)* What did baby Brute find?

b) Where did he find it?

c) How did he feel after he picked it up?

7 Do you think the story will end happily? Say why.

SENTENCE

Rewrite the sentences below. Put in the missing commas like this:

The Brutes were nasty unkind mean and miserable.

The Brutes were nasty, unkind, mean and miserable.

1 My favourite colours are red blue green yellow and orange.

2 I like apples bananas pears peaches and grapes.

3 For her birthday the girl got some skates paints a book and a dress.

4 The road was crowded with bikes cars buses and lorries.

5 In the front room there was a table chairs a settee and a television.

6 There were cows sheep goats pigs and chickens on the farm.

7 Would you like carrots potatoes cabbage peas or sprouts?

WORD

1 Copy the table below. Write the words in the box in the correct columns. Sort the words into how they sound.

ea (long sound) as in l**ea**f	**ea** (short sound) as in h**ea**d
each	dead

each	dead	heavy	great	scream	break
thread	sweat	eat	dear	clear	hear

2 Choose three words from each column. Write one sentence containing each word.

9

The Guest

Owl was at home.

"How good it feels to be sitting by this fire," said Owl. "It is so cold and snowy outside." Owl was eating buttered toast and hot pea soup for supper. Owl heard a loud sound at the front door. "Who is there, banging and pounding at my door on a night like this?" he said.

Owl opened the door. No one was there. Only the snow and the wind. Owl sat near the fire again. There was another loud noise at the door. "Who can it be," said Owl, "knocking and thumping at my door on a night like this?" Owl opened the door. No one was there. Only the snow and the cold. "The poor old winter is knocking at my door," said Owl. "Perhaps it wants to sit by the fire. Well I will be kind and let the winter come in."

Owl opened his door very wide. "Come in, Winter," said Owl. "Come in and warm yourself for a while."

Winter came into the house. It came in very fast. A cold wind pushed Owl against the wall. Winter ran around the room. It blew out the fire in the fireplace. The snow swirled up the stairs and whooshed down the hallway.

"Winter!" cried Owl. "You are my guest. This is no way to behave!"

But Winter did not listen. It made the curtains flap and shiver. It turned the pea soup into hard, green ice. Winter went into all the rooms in Owl's house. Soon everything was covered in snow.

"You must go, Winter!" shouted Owl. "Go away, right now!"

From The Guest *by Arnold Lobel*

TEXT

1 Where does the story take place?

2 Who or what are the two main characters?

3 Which of these words describe Winter?

kind	**nasty**
helpful	**unfriendly**
mischievous	**playful**

4 Do you think the story ended happily? Say why.

5 Say what you liked or disliked about the story.

6 *a)* What is the name of the author?

  b) What is the name of the author of The Brute Family in Unit 3.2?

7 Are the stories similar in any way?

8 Which story did you prefer? Say why.

SENTENCE

Rewrite each sentence. Correct the underlined word in each.

1 The girl climbed over the fence and tore <u>his</u> dress.

2 My brother is silly. <u>She</u> is always getting lost.

3 The pencils <u>was</u> all blunt.

4 The two women went shopping. <u>She</u> bought some apples.

5 I <u>are</u> going to school in the morning.

6 The children <u>has</u> forgotten their books.

7 We <u>was</u> getting wet in the rain.

8 Where <u>is</u> your shoes?

WORD

1 Write these words in two sets according to the **ow** sound.

owl	**how**	**snow**	**blow**	**now**	**grow**
throw	**howl**	**allow**	**know**	**mow**	**crown**

2 Copy these pairs of words. Underline the common spelling pattern in each. The first one has been done for you.

  a) <u>kind</u> <u>wind</u>   *b)* were there   *c)* said paid   *d)* push rush

  e) home come   *f)* near heard   *g)* round you   *h)* one gone

3 Now make up one sentence for each of the words above. Show that you know how to use the words.

Playing with Words

Tongue Twisters

Round and round the rugged rock the ragged rascal ran.

Swan swam over the sea –
Swim, swan, swim!
Swan swam back again –
Well swum swan!

Humorous Rhymes

The elephant carries a great big trunk,
But he never packs it with clothes;
It has no lock and has no key,
But he takes it wherever he goes.

One fine October morning
In September, last July,
The moon lay thick upon the ground,
The snow shone in the sky.
The flowers were singing merrily
The birds were in full bloom
I went down to the cellar
To sweep the upstairs room.

'What am I?' Riddles

My first is in CAT but not in DOG,
My second is in SNOW and also in FOG,
My last is in WHY and also in HOW,
My whole is an animal known as a _ _ _ .

I have four legs but cannot walk.
My back aches when you are comfortable.

TEXT

1 a) Do you think 'tongue twisters' is a good name for some of the sentences oppposite? Why?

b) Which tongue twister did you like best? Why?

2 Write the answers to the two riddles.

3 Which riddle was hardest to work out?

4 Explain what a riddle is.

5 What does 'humorous' mean?

6 Write two sentences to show you know the two meanings of 'trunk'.

7 The second humorous rhyme is called a nonsense rhyme. Why is this?

8 Write the pairs of words that rhyme in the humorous verses.

SENTENCE

Rewrite these sentences. Put in the missing question marks.

Then write a sensible answer for each.

1 who ran round the rugged rock

2 what carries a great big trunk

3 where did the swan swim

4 when is your birthday

5 who sat on a wall and had a great fall

6 what did you do last night

7 where do you live

8 when do you need an umbrella

WORD

1 What is meant by: **a)** a rhyme? **b)** a poem? **c)** a verse?

2 Write when you would use:

a) a full stop **b)** a comma **c)** a question mark

3 Write another word that means the same as:

a) big   **b)** shut   **c)** happy   **d)** good   **e)** shout   **f)** small

4 Write a word that means the opposite of:

a) hot   **b)** near   **c)** thin   **d)** up   **e)** left   **f)** empty

Use the glossary on pages 30–31.

Animal Language

At tea time, when the dog, Jip, came in, the parrot said to the Doctor, 'See, *he's* talking to you.'

'Looks to me as though he were scratching his ear,' said the Doctor.

'But animals don't always speak with their mouths,' said the parrot in a high voice, raising her eyebrows. 'They talk with their ears, with their feet, with their tails – with everything. Sometimes they don't *want* to make a noise. Do you see now the way he's twitching up one side of his nose?'

'What's that mean?' asked the Doctor.

'That means "Can't you see it's stopped raining?" ' Polynesia answered. 'He is asking you a question. Dogs nearly always use their noses for asking questions.'

After a while, with the parrot's help, the Doctor got to learn the language of the animals so well that he could talk to them himself and understand everything they said. Then he gave up being a people's doctor altogether…

As soon as the other animals found out that he could talk their language they told him where the pain was and how they felt, and of course it was easy for him to cure them.

Now all these animals went back and told their brothers and friends that there was a doctor in the little house with the big garden that really was a doctor. And whenever any creatures got sick – not only horses and cows and dogs, but all the little things in the fields, like harvest mice and water voles, badgers and bats – they came at once to his house on the edge of the town, so that his big garden was nearly always crowded with animals trying to get in to see him.

From The Story of Doctor Dolittle *by Hugh Lofting*

TEXT

1 Fill in the gaps with suitable words. Then write the answers.

a) The name of the doctor was Doctor _____.

b) The name of the dog was _____.

c) The name of the parrot was _____.

d) The parrot said that dogs use their _____ for asking questions.

2 What do you know about the house in which the Doctor lived?

3 Can parrots *really* talk or only copy what people say?

4 What sort of man do you think the Doctor was? (For example, was he kind?)

5 In what way are the animals in this story like the Owl in Unit 3.3?

6 What is the name of the author of the story?

7 Say what you liked or disliked about the story.

8 Do you think vets understand animals better than other people do? Why?

SENTENCE

1 Write the questions that are:

a) asking for help   *b)* asking the time   *c)* asking someone to be quiet

Excuse me. Do you have the right time, please?

Can you tell me what the time is?

What's the time?

Would you mind keeping quiet, please?

I'm stuck on this sum. Could you show me what to do?

Can you tell me the way to the High Street?

Can you help me? I've hurt my leg.

Can you make less noise, please?

How can I work if you make all that noise?

WORD

1 Add 'ly' to the end of these words. The first has been done for you.

a) near + ly = nearly   *b)* quick + ly = _____   *c)* slow + ly = _____

2 Now add 'ly' to the end of these words. The first has been done for you.

a) happy + ly = happily   *b)* merry + ly = _____   *c)* easy + ly = _____

3 Add 'ful' to the end of these words. The first has been done for you.

a) care + ful = careful   *b)* help + ful = _____   *c)* use + ful = _____

4 Now write down five more words that end in: *a)* ly *b)* ful

15

Winnie-the-Pooh

Have you ever read any Winnie-the-Pooh stories or poems?
This information about Winnie-the-Pooh, and the men who wrote
and illustrated the books, was taken from the cover of this book.

Winnie-the-Pooh made his first appearance in a poem called 'Teddy Bear' by A. A. Milne, which appeared in *Punch* magazine, in 1923. A. A. Milne's verses were later published in the collection, *When We Were Very Young*, in 1924. The illustrator, E. H. Shepard, was an inspired choice, and the book quickly became a favourite with both young and adult readers.

When, in 1926, A. A. Milne's first stories about Winnie-the-Pooh were published, the book was an instant success. Since then, Winnie-the-Pooh has become a world-famous bear, with A. A. Milne's stories about Pooh and his forest friends translated into thirty-one different languages.

This beautiful edition contains the stories by A. A. Milne from *Winnie-the-Pooh* 1926, and *The House at Pooh Corner* 1928, and the poems from *When We Were Very Young* 1924, and *Now We Are Six* 1927.

The characters of Pooh, Piglet, Eeyore, Tigger, Kanga and Roo, are based upon the real nursery toys belonging to A. A. Milne's son, Christopher Robin, and their adventures are set in the Ashdown Forest where Milne and his family lived. The artist, E. H. Shepard, lovingly depicted the Forest and the toys in his drawings and the places he drew can still be seen today.

From Winnie-the-Pooh – The Complete Collection of Stories and Poems *by A. A. Milne*

TEXT

1 a) Who wrote the stories and poems about Winnie-the-Pooh?

b) Who illustrated them?

2 When did Winnie-the-Pooh first appear?

3 When were the stories about Winnie-the-Pooh first published?

4 How many different languages have the stories been written in?

5 Who are the main characters in the stories?

6 What are the characters based on?

7 Where are the stories set?

8 Why do you think A. A. Milne set the stories in Ashdown Forest?

9 What did you find most interesting about Winnie-the-Pooh?

SENTENCE

Here are the answers to some questions. Write what you think the questions were.

Do it like this:

A. The author of Winnie-the-Pooh was A. A. Milne.

Q. *Who wrote Winnie-the-Pooh?*

1 Ben lives in Luton.

2 Sam likes curry for her dinner.

3 Sonia threw the ball.

4 Dirag went shopping on Monday.

5 Jack is going to the market.

6 Shireen's favourite colour is blue.

7 I am going to Spain on holiday.

8 My teacher's name is Mrs Shahidi.

9 It is nine o'clock.

10 Ali is going to the park.

WORD

Longer words may be broken into smaller parts.
These parts are called syllables.
bear is made of one syllable
hedge/hog is made of two syllables
el/e/phant is made of three syllables
Say the words in the box aloud and listen carefully.

| his | we | quickly | later | adventure | famous |
| book | story | contain | toy | collection | artist |

1 Which of the words in the box are made of one syllable?

2 Which of the words are made of two syllables?

3 Which of the words are made of three syllables?

4 Write down two types of fruit which have one syllable.

5 Write down two types of fruit which have two syllables.

6 Can you write down a fruit or vegetable which has three syllables?

The Jungle Book

This is the story of how the boy Mowgli was brought up in the jungle. When Mowgli was a baby, he was saved from a tiger and bought up by a pair of wolves, with help from Baloo, a sleepy old brown bear, and Bagheera, a black panther.

Mowgli grew up with the wolf cubs, though they, of course, were grown wolves almost before he was a child, and Father Wolf taught him his business, and the meaning of things in the Jungle, till every rustle in the grass, every breath of the warm night air, every note of the owls above his head, every scratch of a bat's claws as it roosted for a while in a tree, and every splash of every little fish jumping in a pool, meant just as much to him as the work of his office means to a business man.

When he was not learning, Mowgli sat out in the sun and slept, and ate and went to sleep again; when he felt dirty or hot he swam in the forest pools; and when he wanted honey (Baloo told him that nuts and honey were just as pleasant to eat as raw meat) he climbed up for it, and that Bagheera showed him how to do. Bagheera would lie out on a branch and call, 'Come along, Little Brother,' and at first Mowgli would cling like a sloth, but afterward he would fling himself through the branches almost as boldly as the grey ape.

Mowgli took his place at the Council Rock, too, when the Pack met, and there he discovered that if he stared hard enough at any wolf, the wolf would be forced to drop his eyes, and so he used to stare for fun.
At other times he would pluck the long thorns out of the pads of his friends, for wolves suffer terribly from thorns and burrs in their coats.

From The Jungle Book
by Rudyard Kipling

TEXT

1 Is Mowgli a boy or an animal? How can you tell?

2 Where did Mowgli live? How can you tell?

3 List some of the things Mowgli learned.

4 What did Mowgli do when he felt hot or dirty?

5 *a)* Who is Baloo?

b) Who is Bagheera?

c) How did they help Mowgli?

6 When Mowgli stared at any wolf it would 'drop its eyes'. What does this mean?

7 How did Mowgli help the wolves?

8 In what ways are the story in Unit 3.5 and the story in this Unit similar?

SENTENCE

Copy the sentences. Fill in each gap with the correct form of the verb. The first one has been done for you.

1 Mowgli was __brought__ up in the jungle. (bring)

2 Mowgli _____ up with the wolf cubs. (grow)

3 Father Wolf _____ Mowgli lots of things. (teach)

4 When he was not learning, Mowgli _____ in the sun. (sit)

5 Last night he _____ under a tree. (sleep)

6 Yesterday he _____ some nuts. (eat)

7 When he _____ hot, Mowgli had a swim. (feel)

8 Mowgli _____ in the forest pools. (swim)

WORD

1 Find a word in the story containing these spelling patterns:

a) ough   *b)* augh   *c)* igh   *d)* ace   *e)* ice   *f)* ould

g) are   *h)* ild   *i)* ey   *j)* ie   *k)* ei   *l)* oa

2 Find a word in the story containing:

a) ch   *b)* tch   *c)* sh   *d)* wh

3 Find a word in the story beginning with:

a) cl__   *b)* fl__   *c)* pl__   *d)* sl__   *e)* br__

f) dr__   *g)* fr__   *h)* gr__   *i)* scr__   *j)* sw__

4 Find a word in the story ending in:

a) __ld   *b)* __le   *c)* __lf   *d)* __lt   *e)* __ly

Veterinary Surgeon

Veterinary surgeon

I am a veterinary surgeon and I treat sick animals. I examine cats, dogs, and other small pets in my surgery. And if a cow or horse is unwell, I go by car to visit it on the farm. Then I give it medicine to make it well.

Vets visits
People carry their pets to surgery in baskets so they don't run away.

Difficult patients
Sometimes vets visit unusual patients in zoos. These animals may be too dangerous to treat when awake. Lions often have to be tranquillised first.

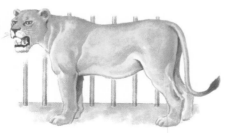

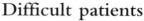

muzzle

scissors

clippers

ear torch

Vets' instruments
Vets' instruments help them treat sick animals. Animals must keep still and not bite. To stop a dog biting, the vet may use a muzzle.

At the farm
Vets may treat whole herds of cows. To stop them catching and spreading an illness, they may all be injected on one day.

At the surgery
Pets wait in the waiting room for the vet to see them.

A sick cat
During a check-up, the vet asks how the animal is behaving. He then examines the animal to find out what is wrong.

From Jobs People Do *by Christopher Maynard*

T E X T

1 What job does the page opposite tell you about?

2 Is it a page from a fiction or a non-fiction book?

3 Copy and complete the following facts about a veterinary surgeon:

   a) A veterinary surgeon treats sick _____.

   b) A vet examines small animals in a _____.

   c) Sometimes a vet has to visit a _____ to treat cows or horses.

   d) People carry their pets to the surgery in _____.

   e) One instrument a vet uses is called _____.

   f) Sometimes dangerous animals have to be _____.

4 Which fact about vets did you find most interesting? Why?

5 How do the pictures on the page help you?

6 How do the headings on the page help you?

7 Did the page help you learn more about vets?

8 Think of one question you would like to ask a vet about his or her job.

S E N T E N C E

Make up eight questions of your own about veterinary surgeons. (You do not have to write the answers!) Make sure each question ends with a question mark.

Try to use the words **what**, **when**, **who** and **where** in your questions.

Write the questions like this: *Where does a vet work?*

W O R D

1 Write five words you have learned about the job of a vet.

  Write what each word means. Do it like this:

  veterinary surgeon – a veterinary surgeon is an animal doctor.

2 Write another word that means the same as:

   a) sick   *b)* wrong   *c)* basket   *d)* run away   *e)* bite

   f) see   *g)* examine *h)* find out   *i)* surgeon   *j)* look after

Using an Information Book

Here are parts of three pages from an information book on cats. Knowing how to use these pages will help you a great deal.

Contents

A contents page tells you what sections the book is divided into. It comes at the beginning of a book.

Index

An index tells you where to find specific things. It comes near the end of the book.

Glossary

grooming brushing and combing your cat

injections cats have to be vaccinated/injected by a vet to stop them catching diseases.

litter new born kittens

A glossary tells you the meaning of hard words. It comes near the end of a book.

From Cats *by Michaela Miller*

TEXT

1 a) What does a contents page tell you? **b)** Where does it come in a book?

2 a) What does an index tell you? **b)** Where does it come in a book?

3 a) What would you find in a glossary?

b) Where would you find a glossary in a book?

4 Use the contents page opposite. On which page would you find:

a) feeding time? **b)** keeping clean? **c)** the index?

5 Use the index on the opposite page. On which page or pages would you find information on:

a) kittens? **b)** fleas? **c)** a vet? **d)** playing?

6 Use the glossary to explain what each of these mean:

a) grooming **b)** litter **c)** injections

7 On which page of this Activity Book (that you are working from) can you find:

a) the contents page? **b)** the glossary?

SENTENCE

Rewrite each sentence. Correct the underlined word so it makes sense.

1 I think cats <u>is</u> very nice.

2 They <u>has</u> soft fur and whiskers.

3 A cat <u>like</u> to drink milk.

4 There <u>was</u> lots of cats in the garden.

5 One cat <u>were</u> chasing a bird.

6 My cat and dog <u>is</u> great friends.

7 They <u>goes</u> everywhere together.

8 My dad <u>give</u> me a pet.

WORD

1 Copy these words. Underline a small word within each one. The first one has been done for you.

a) p<u>art</u>s **b)** pages **c)** great **d)** where **e)** healthy **f)** what
g) feeding **h)** kittens **i)** brush **j)** catching **k)** disease **l)** combing

2 Find a word on page 22 that contains the letters:

a) nn **b)** ss **c)** tt **d)** cc

e) ll **f)** ee **g)** oo

3 Make up some sentences of your own. Use each of the words you found for question 2 in your sentences.

The Silly Ghosts Gruff

Once there were three ghosts. They were called the Silly Ghosts Gruff. There was Little Silly Ghost Gruff, Big Silly Ghost Gruff and Piddle-sized Silly Ghost Gruff. And they all lived in a field by a river. One day they thought they would like to cross the river to eat the grass on the other side.

Now, over this river there was a fridge and underneath this fridge was a horrible roll. A horrible Cheese roll. So the Little Silly Ghost Gruff, he stepped on the fridge, drip, drop, drip, drop, over the fridge; when suddenly, there on the fridge was the horrible roll.

'I'm a roll-foll-de-roll and you'll eat me up for your supper!'

'Oh no, oh no, oh no,' said Little Silly Ghost Gruff. 'I don't want to eat you. My big brother the Piddle-sized Silly Ghost Gruff is going to be coming along soon and he can eat you for his supper.'

'Very well,' said the horrible roll, 'you can cross the fridge.' And drip, drop, drip, drop, over the fridge went the Little Silly Ghost Gruff.

Exactly the same thing happened to the Piddle-sized Silly Ghost Gruff.

Then along comes the Big Silly Ghost Gruff. Drip, drop, drip, drop, over the fridge, and, suddenly, there was the horrible roll again.

'I'm a roll-foll-de-roll and you'll eat me up for your supper!'

'Oh can I? Oh can I?' said the Big Silly Ghost Gruff. And at that he ran at the horrible roll and went straight through it (he was a ghost, don't forget). And so over the fridge he went drip, drop, drip, drop, till he got to the other side.

And from that day on, no roll, no cheese roll, or ham roll or even jam roll ever bothered the Silly Ghosts Gruff again.

The Silly Ghosts Gruff (slightly adapted) *from* Hairy Tales and Nursery Crimes *by Michael Rosen*

TEXT

1 Copy the sentences. Fill in the gaps.

a) There were once three _____ _____ _____.

b) They lived in a _____ by a _____.

c) Over the river there was a _____.

d) Under the fridge lived a horrible _____.

e) The Big Silly Ghost Gruff ran straight _____ the horrible roll.

2 *a)* What story does this one remind you of?

b) Who is the horrible Cheese roll like? *c)* What is the fridge like?

3 Did you like the story? Say what you liked or disliked about it.

4 Which story do you like best – the original story or this one? Why?

5 The author has had fun playing with words in this story. Write what you think 'playing with words' means.

SENTENCE

Rewrite each sentence. Put in the missing capital letters, full stops, commas and question marks.

1 the author of the silly ghosts gruff was michael rosen

2 did the story make you laugh

3 in the fridge there was a sandwich a roll some cheese and milk

4 what was on the other side of the river

5 there is a big bridge over the river thames

6 on the river there are rowing boats fishing ships and yachts

7 have you ever been to london

8 mrs shah had a cat called smudge

WORD

1 Find and write the words from the story hidden in the letters. The first one has been done for you.

a) a b g h o s t

b) k r i v e r m b

c) f r i d g e w f h

d) z x f i e l d v b

e) b v d s g r a s s

f) z w q r o l l g h j

g) s u p p e r j n d

h) h o r r i b l e f s

i) q t y c r o s s u o

2 Now make up some sentences of your own. Include each of the words you found in them.

1. Finishing a story

1 Read Unit 3.1 again.

Mrs Mudd asks everyone to help her make an apple pie.

◆ Write what everybody says.
Mrs Mudd asks everyone if they would like to share her apple pie.

◆ Write what everybody says.

◆ What does Mrs Mudd reply?

2 Read Unit 2.2 again.

Baby Brute takes the good feeling home with him.

◆ What happens? How does everyone change?

◆ What sort of things do the Brutes do and say?

2. Writing a story

Beginning

It's a lovely day for a walk.

Let's cross the bridge.

William and Sarah went for a walk along the river bank.

Middle

Get off my bridge!

Help! It must be the ugly troll!

When they crossed the bridge an ugly monster jumped up.

End

How will the story end?

Remember – every story should have a good beginning, middle and end!

◆ Make this into a longer story.

◆ Remember to include what people say and do.

◆ Explain how they feel.

◆ Use interesting words to make it exciting.

3. Other ideas for stories

◆ Write about a funny or strange adventure Dr Dolittle has (Unit 3.5).

◆ Imagine you are Mowgli. Write a story about an adventure you have in the jungle with your animal friends (Unit 3.7).

4. Writing a nonsense verse

Imagine every child in your class met a funny creature on their way to school. Write what they would say. Here are some ideas to start with.

Why not have a go at writing a tongue twister or a riddle, too?

On my way to school, I met a bear with long curly hair.	On my way to school, I met a fox with stripy socks.	On my way to school, I met a crocodile with a wicked smile.

5. Writing an information text

Here are some notes about machines you see on a building site.

Write some proper sentences about each machine.

Give each set of sentences a heading.

Draw a picture of each machine.

The crane
strong metal cable – metal hook – lifts heavy things – operator controls crane – sits in cab – crane driven by motor – some cranes enormous

The mechanical digger
giant shovel on an arm at front – digs big holes very quickly and easily – driver sits in cab with controls – two steel legs at front stop digger from tipping when digging

The bulldozer
scrapes ground level – shovels up earth – diesel engine – no wheels – steel 'caterpillar' tracks help over rough ground

How are you getting on with the skills in the chart?
If you need extra practice, try the activities shown.

Grammar and punctuation	Writing sensible sentences	1
	Questions	2
	General punctuation	3
Spelling, phonics and vocabulary	Phonemes	4
	Spelling patterns	5
	Words with similar meanings	6
	Suffixes with 'ly' and 'ful'	7
	Syllables	8
	Spelling strategies	9/10

1 Rewrite these sentences correctly.

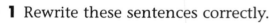

a) Cats likes drinking milk.
b) A snakes like to hiss.
c) The farmers was driving a tractor.
d) The bag were full of sweets.
e) My house have a big garden.
f) The girl were writing with a pencil belonging to his father.

2 Here are some answers. Write what you think the questions were.

a) My name is Sally.
b) I would like an apple, please.
c) I'm lost.
d) I like pizza best.
e) It's nearly time for dinner.
f) It was Tom at the door.

3 Copy these sentences. Punctuate them correctly.

a) where are you going
b) sam gave ben one of her sweets
c) how did you do that
d) the old lady was carrying a heavy bag
e) mrs smith likes apples bananas pears and grapes
f) it was a nice day the sun was very hot

4 Think of a suitable phoneme to finish each word.

a) t __ __ l
b) p__ __ t
c) cl __ __
d) fl __ __
e) f __ __ l
f) __ __ t
g) m __ __ n
h) r __ __ nd

5 Write the words in each box in two sets according to their sounds:

> **ow**: cow low how grow mow now

> **ea**: bead read head bread plead dead

6 Match up each word from Set A to a word with a similar meaning in Set B.

Set A	cunning	wet	fast	high	feeble	broad
Set B	tall	weak	wide	sly	damp	quick

7 Add 'ful' or 'ly' to the end of these words.

a) help<u>ful</u>   *b)* slow___   *c)* love___

d) cheer____   *e)* care___   *f)* quick___

g) sad___   *h)* hope____

8 Copy these words. Write how many syllables each word contains. Do it like this: red (1)

a) yellow   *b)* banana   *c)* apple

d) blue   *e)* ruler   *f)* rainbow

g) elephant   *h)* they   *i)* volcano

9 Look at the words on page 32. Find two words beginning with:

a) a   **b)** d   *c)* f   **d)** o   *e)* s   *f)* w

10 Look at the words on page 32. Find:

a) five words with two letters

b) ten words with three letters

c) five words with four letters

d) four words with six letters

Handy hints for spelling words

> **Look** – Look carefully at the word.

> **Say** – Say the word to hear how it sounds.

> **Cover** – Cover the word and try to see it in your mind.

> **Write** – Write the word from memory.

> **Check** – Check your spelling.

Glossary

author

An **author** is someone who writes books.

capital letter

1. A sentence always begins with a **capital letter**.

2. Special names, like people's names and names of the days and months, also begin with a **capital letter**.

3. **Capital letters** are sometimes used to make words stand out.

character

Characters are the names of people, animals or things that appear in stories.

comma

A **comma** is a punctuation mark. It tells you to pause.
It is also used to separate items in a list.

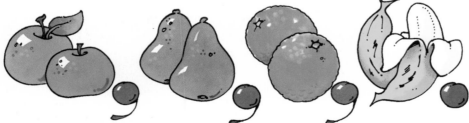

I like apples, pears, oranges and bananas.

contents page

A **contents page** appears at the beginning of a book.
It tells you the names of the sections or chapters in the book.

fact

A **fact** is something that is true.

fiction

A **fiction** story is one which has not really happened.
It is made up.
Non-fiction books are about things that are true.

full stop

A **full stop** is a dot showing that a sentence has ended.

glossary

A **glossary** is a list of special words and their meanings.

index

An **index** is a list at the end of a book, telling you on which pages to find particular things.

opposite

Opposites are two words whose meanings are as different as possible from each other

hot   cold

phoneme

A **phoneme** is the smallest unit of sound in a word. It may be made up of one, two, three or four letters, e.g. t**o**, sh**oe**, thr**ough**

punctuation

Punctuation helps us make sense of what we read. Punctuation marks make writing easier for us to understand. Full stops, commas, question marks and exclamation marks are all punctuation marks.

question

May I stay up and watch the late film?
A **question** is what we ask when we want to know something. Questions always end with a question mark.

rhyme

A **rhyme** occurs when two words have an ending that sounds the same.

h**ead**   b**ed**

riddle

A **riddle** is a word puzzle to be solved.

sentence

A **sentence** should make sense on its own. It should begin with a capital letter. Most sentences end with a full stop.

spelling pattern

A **spelling pattern** is a group of letters which occur often in words, e.g. l**ight** br**ight** fr**ight**

syllable

Longer words may be broken down into smaller parts called **syllables**.

'bad' has one syllable
'bad/min/ton' has three syllables

tongue twister

A **tongue twister** is something you have difficulty saying. The words often begin with the same sound.

'Peter Piper picked a peck of pickled peas' is a tongue twister.

verb

A **verb** is a doing word, e.g.
A dog **barks**.

verse

A poem is often divided into parts, or **verses**.

High frequency word list

about
after
again
an
another
as

back
ball
be
because
bed
been
boy
brother
but
by

call(ed)
came
can't could

did
dig
do
don't
door
down

first
from

girl
good
got

had
half
has
have

help
her
here
him
his
home
house
how

if

jump
just

last
laugh
little
live(d)
love

made
make
man
many
may
more
much
must

name
new
next
night
not
now

off
old
once
one

or
our
out
over

people
pull
push
put

ran

saw
school
seen
should
sister
so
some

take
than
that
their
them
then
there
these
three
time
too
took
tree
two

us

very

want
water

way
were
what
when
where
who
will
with
would

your

Days of the week:
Monday
Tuesday
Wednesday
Thursday
Friday
Saturday
Sunday

Months:
January
February
March
April
May
June
July
August
September
October
November
December

Colours:
black
blue
brown
green
pink
orange
purple
red
white
yellow

Numbers to twenty:
one
two
three
four
five
six
seven
eight
nine
ten
eleven
twelve
thirteen
fourteen
fifteen
sixteen
seventeen
eighteen
nineteen
twenty